Spotlight on
ANCIENT CIVILIZATIONS
EGYPT

Ancient Egyptian CULTURE

Leigh Rockwood

Published in 2014 by The Rosen Publishing Group, Inc.
29 East 21st Street, New York, NY 10010

First Edition

Editor: Jennifer Way
Book Design: Kate Vlachos
Layout Design: Colleen Bialecki

Photo Credits: Cover Ian Cumming/Axiom Photographic Agency/Getty Images; p. 4 Ksenia Palimski/Shutterstock.com; p. 5 Sadequl Hussain/Shutterstock.com; p. 6 SuperStock/Getty Images; pp. 7, 14, 18, 19 (left) Egyptian/The Bridgeman Art Library/Getty Images; p. 8 Nomad_Soul/Shutterstock.com; pp. 9, 19 DEA/G. Dagli Orti/De Agostini Picture Library; pp. 10, 11 (top), 16, 17, 19 (right) DEA Picture Library/De Agostini Picture Library/Getty Images; pp. 11 (bottom), 21 © 2001 Francis Dzikowski; pp. 12–13 sculpies/Shutterstock.com; p. 15 Zhukov Oleg/Shutterstock.com; p. 20 EugenZ/Shutterstock.com; p. 22 Francisco Javier Gil/Shutterstock.com.

Library of Congress Cataloging-in-Publication Data

Rockwood, Leigh.
 Ancient Egyptian culture / by Leigh Rockwood. — 1st ed.
    p. cm. — (Spotlight on ancient civilizations: Egypt)
Includes index.
 ISBN 978-1-4777-0763-0 (library binding) — ISBN 978-1-4777-0859-0 (pbk.) — ISBN 978-1-4777-0860-6 (6-pack)
 1. Egypt—Civilization—To 332 B.C.—Juvenile literature. 2. Egypt—Social life and customs—To 332 B.C.—Juvenile literature. I. Title. II. Series: Spotlight on ancient civilizations. Egypt.
 DT61.R535 2014
 932.01—dc23
                                    2012044924

Manufactured in the United States of America

CPSIA Compliance Information: Batch #S13PK2: For Further Information contact Rosen Publishing, New York, New York at 1-800-237-9932

CONTENTS

Ancient Egyptian Culture

Ancient Egyptian **civilization** lasted from about 3100 BC until 332 BC. This civilization's **culture** was shaped in large part by its religion. Religion influenced how the ancient Egyptian people understood and interacted with the world around them. People believed that there were numerous gods and goddesses and that they controlled everything, including animals, crops, and even the Sun itself.

Tombs and temples in ancient Egypt had their walls painted with scenes that honored and told stories about gods and rulers. This painting shows a king (right) and Thoth (left), the god of knowledge.

Ancient Egyptians often depicted their gods in animal form. Here is a statue of the god Horus in the form of a falcon.

Ancient Egyptians honored their gods through artwork, such as sculptures and paintings in tombs and **temples**. People believed that if the gods were honored, they would help people both in life and after death. The art that ancient Egyptians left behind tells us detailed stories about the culture, history, and beliefs of this civilization.

Creation Myths

Creation myths exist in almost every culture. These are stories that describe how the world was formed, where the gods came from, and how civilization began. Each of the four major cities of ancient Egypt had its own creation myth, and each focused on different gods. These cities were Hermopolis, Heliopolis, Memphis, and Thebes.

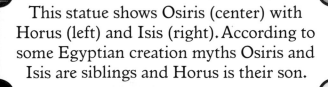

This statue shows Osiris (center) with Horus (left) and Isis (right). According to some Egyptian creation myths Osiris and Isis are siblings and Horus is their son.

Atum (right) is the god of creation in the earliest Egyptian myths based in the city of Heliopolis. In this tomb painting, he is telling Osiris (left) that one day he will destroy the world that he created.

Ancient Egyptian creation myths had some things in common, though. They all said that the world was created from an ocean of darkness and that a pyramid-shaped mound arose from this water. Then different gods appeared and formed elements such as the Earth, the Sun, and the sky.

Gods and Goddesses

Each of Egypt's main regions honored its own set of gods. Over time, some gods were honored throughout Egypt or became linked with local gods. For example, the Sun god Ra became associated with the Sun gods of other regions.

The major center of worship of the Sun god Ra was in Heliopolis, where he was identified with that city's Sun god Atum. Ra took on many forms in ancient Egyptian art. Here he has the head of a falcon.

In Memphis, Ptah was worshipped as the god of creation. People there believed that Ptah created Ra. Ptah was worshipped in other parts of ancient Egypt as the god of craftsmen.

By around 2500 BC, Egypt's **pharaohs**, or rulers, were linked to its religion. The pharaoh was associated with the god Horus and was believed to be the human form of that god. Horus was shown as a falcon or as a man with a falcon's head. He was a god of the sky and the ruler of the Earth.

9

The Afterlife

The afterlife, or the belief in life after death, was important to ancient Egyptian culture. The ancient Egyptians built tombs to house the dead. People filled these tombs with food, clothing, and other things that their loved ones needed for the afterlife.

Once a body was mummified, a burial mask was placed over the head. This was believed to guard the person's soul on the way to the afterlife. This is the pharaoh Tutankhamen's burial mask. He lived from around 1342 BC until 1323 BC.

Preserving bodies after death was a long-standing practice in ancient Egypt. In this tomb painting, Anubis is shown tending to a mummy. Anubis is the god of the afterlife.

Mummies were placed in burial chambers within tombs. This is the burial chamber of Twosret and Setnakhte, in the Valley of the Kings, near Luxor, Egypt.

Ancient Egyptians believed that **preserving** a person's body after death made him able to enjoy the afterlife. A preserved body is called a **mummy**. A mummy was made by drying the body out and then wrapping it in cloth. After the mummy was prepared, a priest performed **rituals** before the mummy was put in its final resting place.

11

Architecture and Culture

The main building materials in ancient Egyptian **architecture** were sunbaked mud bricks and stone, such as sandstone, limestone, and granite. Settlements were built of mud bricks near the fertile Nile River valley. These buildings were destroyed over time either through reuse or by the flooding of the Nile.

The ancient Egyptian structures that still stand today were made of stone and were often built on higher, drier land than other buildings. These structures tell us much of what we know about this civilization's culture. The pyramids were tombs that honored the pharaohs. There were temples built to honor and house gods, as well as to honor pharaohs.

The Pyramids of Giza, shown here, were built around 5,000 years ago. The three main pyramids were built to be the burial sites for the pharaohs Khufu, Khafre, and Menkaure.

Rituals

Temple rituals were important in ancient Egyptian culture. There were daily rituals for the gods at dawn, at midday, and at sunset. As part of these rituals, statues of the gods were clothed and were made offerings of food and drink.

This painting from the tomb of Ramses shows a priest making an offering.

The Karnak Temple Complex contains temples that stretch across ancient Egyptian history. Building began here around 2100 BC and continued through the end of ancient Egyptian civilization.

Ancient Egyptians believed that the pharaoh was the only person who could speak to the gods directly. Of course, it was not possible for the pharaoh to perform daily rituals at every temple in Egypt. Priests performed temple rituals as representatives for the pharaoh. Ordinary Egyptians did not take part in temple rituals. Instead, they made offerings to the gods at home.

Magic

Magic and religion were closely linked in ancient Egyptian culture. People believed that they could keep away sickness or bring good luck with magic spells and special charms. The Book of the Dead was placed in people's tombs and contained magic spells to help the dead on their journey through the afterlife. Egyptians believed that the gods decided whether or not these spells worked.

This jeweled breastplate has a scarab at the center. The scarab beetle was a symbol of the Sun god Ra and of the cycle of life.

Here is a page from the Book of the Dead. This book of spells for the afterlife was printed on paper made from the papyrus plant.

People often wore small **amulets** on bracelets or necklaces to act as charms. These amulets were also buried with the dead to protect them in the afterlife. Amulets often looked like animals that held symbolic meaning.

Music and Dance

Both music and dancing were found throughout ancient Egyptian culture. People danced to praise the gods for providing good harvests. Musicians played during feasts as well as during ceremonies in temples. Common instruments in ancient Egypt included flutes, harps, trumpets, and drums. These instruments have all been found in tombs.

This painting from the tomb of a nobleman shows women playing music.

This trumpet (left), shown with its wooden stopper (right), was buried with the pharaoh Tutankhamen.

Drum

The pharaohs often had musicians and dancers perform at their palace. Decorations in tombs and temples show us that it was mainly women who were musicians and dancers. These show scenes of women dancing and playing instruments.

Art and Hieroglyphics

In ancient Egypt, art was used to honor both the pharaoh and the gods. Sculptures and statues were created for this purpose. **Obelisks**, which are tall, pointed monuments covered in **hieroglyphics**, were placed at temple entrances. Art, wall paintings, furniture, and finely crafted jewelry filled pharaohs' tombs for the pharaoh to enjoy in the afterlife.

The Great Sphinx of Giza, shown here, has a human head and a lion's body. It is one of the world's oldest monuments. It was built about 4,600 years ago!

The owl shown in this hieroglyph stood for the sound the letter M makes.

Hieroglyphics is the ancient Egyptian system of writing using pictures and other symbols. The earliest-known hieroglyphics date to 3000 BC. By the end of the ancient Egyptian civilization, there were more than 700 different symbols!

What Remains Today

Archaeologists study ancient human history. They look at the mummies, art, temples, tombs, writings, and other things left behind by the ancient Egyptians to understand this civilization. Luckily, Egypt has a very dry climate, which has helped preserve many of these things for thousands of years.

Today, many museums display art and other objects from ancient Egypt. That means that people all over the world can get close-up looks at one of the most fascinating civilizations in human history.

Some ancient Egyptian buildings still stand today. This is a detail from a temple in Abu Simbel, Egypt. Ruins like these help archaeologists and historians understand the culture of this ancient civilization.

GLOSSARY

amulets (AM-yeh-lets) Things worn as good-luck charms.

archaeologists (ahr-kee-AH-luh-jists) People who study the remains of peoples from the past to understand how they lived.

architecture (AR-kih-tek-cher) The art of creating and making buildings.

civilization (sih-vih-lih-ZAY-shun) People living in a certain way.

creation myths (kree-AY-shun MITHS) Stories of how the world came to be and people came to live in it.

culture (KUL-chur) The beliefs, practices, and arts of a group of people.

hieroglyphics (hy-er-uh-GLIF-iks) A form of writing that uses more than 700 pictures for different words and sounds.

mummy (MUH-mee) A body prepared for burial in a way that makes it last a long time.

obelisks (AH-buh-lisks) Tall columns that end in triangular shapes.

pharaohs (FER-ohz) Ancient Egyptian rulers.

preserving (prih-ZURV-ing) Keeping something from being lost or from going bad.

rituals (RIH-choo-ulz) Special actions done for reasons of faith.

temples (TEM-pelz) Places where people go to worship.

INDEX

WEBSITES

Due to the changing nature of Internet links, PowerKids Press has developed an online list of websites related to the subject of this book. This site is updated regularly. Please use this link to access the list: www.powerkidslinks.com/sace/cult/